AF227963

THE LAMP

In Conversation with St. Luke

A Play & Lament in Verse

Presented in Three Acts

SAINT JULIAN PRESS

THE LAMP

In Conversation with St. Luke

A Play & Lament in Verse

Presented in Three Acts

Ron Starbuck

SAINT JULIAN PRESS
HOUSTON

Published by
SAINT JULIAN PRESS, Inc.
2053 Cortlandt, Suite 200
Houston, Texas 77008
www.saintjulianpress.org

Print ISBN-13: 978-1-955194-52-5
eBook ISBN-13: 978-1-955194-53-2
Library of Congress Control Number: 2026935603

Cover Image: *Basilica Cattedrale Patriarcale di San Marco*
The Patriarchal Cathedral Basilica of Saint Mark
Photo by Ron Starbuck from Venice, Italy

ACT I — THE CITY THAT CALLS ITSELF BRIGHT

(Visibility, Dependence, and the Drawing of the Line)

Prologue — The Word Once Spoken

Scene I — Before Dawn

Scene II — The City That Eats and Forgets

Scene III — Daniel Speaks of the City

Scene IV — Policy: The Language of Order

Scene V — Captain Morrow: Ritual Before Duty

Scene VI — Officer Reyes: Inheritance

ACT II — THE LINE

(Confrontation and Catastrophe)

Scene VII — The Gathering

Scene VIII — The Line

Scene IX — The Sound

Scene X — After: The Hope That Does Not Erase

ACT III — NORMALIZATION

ON THE THREE MOVEMENTS

This play moves in three arcs of light.

It begins with visibility — with hands before dawn, with kitchens and concrete, with a city calling itself bright. Nothing has yet shattered. The towers still catch the morning light. Yet even here, a line is forming — quiet, procedural, almost reasonable — between those who are seen and those who are not, but used.

The second movement tightens. Fear assumes a posture. A line becomes a wall; a wall becomes a command. What was language becomes motion. What was written as policy hardens into metal. The act itself is sudden — a misjudgment born of fear. A body falls, and the air changes. The city does not collapse. It inhales — and does not know how to exhale.

The cruelty is not only in the moment. It is in the structure that made the moment possible — in the deterrence accepted as wisdom, in the reflex trained to expect threat, in a system that learns to live with what it has done.

The final movement is softer in tone yet sharper in consequence. The event leaves the street and enters our speech. Language gathers. Words assemble: necessary, law, order. Explanation replaces shock. Justification learns to speak calmly. The question shifts. Not what happened — but what we will permit to continue.

The light of the body is the eye:
therefore when thine eye is single,
thy whole body also is full of light.

— Luke 11:34
King James Version

THE LAMP

A Lament in Verse
For Theater in the Round
After the *Gospel of Luke* 11:34–36

CAST

The Voice — Conscience *(implied as Jesus, never named)*

Miriam — hospitality worker, undocumented

Daniel — her son, 17, born in the city

Captain Morrow — police commander

Officer Reyes — patrol officer, son of immigrants

Mayor — city leader

State Official — state authority

Elijah — organizer

Reporter — the public tongue

Ensemble — Workers / Clergy / Citizens / Officers / Protestors (as assigned)

FORM – Theater in the Round

Each scene begins with an invocation spoken by an actor, a reader, or a rotating ensemble.

Characters then step forward to the center of a chapel or theater in the round *(possibly a stained-glass wash or pool of light)*, speak, and return.

Silence is part of the text.

ACT I — THE CITY THAT CALLS ITSELF BRIGHT

Prologue — The Word Once Spoken

A city is named before it is judged. Light is introduced not as comfort, but as responsibility. Scripture is not quoted as ornament, but as a mirror. The audience is invited to pay attention. Nothing has happened yet — but everything is already at stake.

INVOCATION

A city of glass and labor.

A city of towers and kitchens.

A city that rises before dawn

and sleeps lightly at night.

A city built by hands

that do not always appear in its records.

A city that calls itself bright.

(…silence)

READER

Hear now a word once spoken:

The light of the body is the eye: therefore when thine eye is single, thy whole body also is full of light; but when thine eye is evil, thy body also is full of darkness.

Take heed therefore that the light which is in thee be not darkness.

If thy whole body therefore be full of light, having no part dark, the whole shall be full of light, as when the bright shining of a candle doth give thee light.

— Luke 11:34–36
King James Version

(…long silence—count it)

THE VOICE

You think this is about vision.

It is about permission.

(…silence)

SCENE I — BEFORE DAWN

The city wakes in its hidden hours. Labor begins before visibility.
Those who sustain the brightness of the skyline stand in shadow.
The tone is quiet, factual, unresentful — but aware. The
question beneath the scene: Who rises first, and who is seen last?

INVOCATION

Before sunrise.

Steel against whitening sky.

Coffee in paper cups.

Hands already working.

The day not yet decided.

WORKER 1

Concrete's late.

WORKER 2

Concrete is never late.

It arrives when it wants

and we arrive when it wants

and our backs arrive when it wants.

WORKER 1

They came last night.

To Building C.

Three floors awake at once

like startled birds.

MIRIAM

Three doors open.

Three doors empty.

A fourth door left open

like a mouth.

WORKER 2

This city runs on us.

WORKER 1

This city runs past us.

WORKER 2

The towers catch the morning light

before we do.

THE VOICE

You live among them.

You sleep in what they build.

You eat what they carry.

You heal in what they clean.

You call this economy.

It is dependence

wearing a clean shirt.

SCENE II — THE CITY THAT EATS AND FORGETS

Inside kitchens and service corridors, repetition replaces recognition. The work is essential; the workers are conditional. The mood is restrained, almost rhythmic — the machinery of routine. Conscience interrupts gently: safety is not distributed evenly.

INVOCATION

Stainless steel.

Steam rising.

Orders called in two languages.

A clock louder than conscience.

DISHWASHER (ENSEMBLE)

Order up.

COOK (ENSEMBLE)

Order up.

SERVER (ENSEMBLE)

Smile, smile, smile.

MIRIAM

I scrub rooms.

I empty bins.

I erase the fingerprints

of other people's lives

and call it a job.

They notice dust.

They do not notice

who wipes it away.

THE VOICE

Essential, they say.

But not enough to be safe.

SCENE III — DANIEL SPEAKS OF THE CITY

This is belonging without permission. Daniel speaks not in defiance but in clarity. He loves the city. He claims it. The tone is earnest, intelligent, grounded. The audience must feel what is at risk — not abstractly, but personally.

INVOCATION

A classroom at dusk.

Fluorescent hum.

Lockers closing.

A city held in textbooks.

Outside: traffic like a restless ocean.

DANIEL

I know this city by its bridges.

I know which ones flood

when rain comes hard

and the streets forget their names.

I know which highways split

like arguments—

how one neighborhood becomes two

because someone drew a line

and called it planning.

I know the skyline

from the bus window

and which tower turns gold first

at sunset.

I like the way the skyline holds the light

like it belongs to everyone.

I learned the pledge

before I learned

why my mother lowers her voice

when she says "papers."

In fourth grade

I drew the courthouse

with crayons.

I colored it bright.

The teacher said,

"That's where justice lives."

I believed her.

I believe in things that rise.

I believe in math

because math does not ask

where you were born.

I want to build bridges

that do not care

who crosses.

I want to build something

that stays.

(breath–pause)

They say "illegal."

They say it like a shadow

falls across a face.

But I was born here.

I am an American

born here in this place.

I took my first steps

on this pavement.

I scraped my knees

on this concrete.

I pledged allegiance

in this language.

If this city is not mine,

whose breath

(breath–pause)

have I been breathing

while you were looking away?

When you say "go back,"

tell me—

to which bridge?

Tonight they gather downtown.

Mom says keep my head down.

But my head is where my questions live.

If I lower it,

what happens to the questions?

(breath–pause — he looks into the circle)

If I stand in the street tonight,

I am not trespassing.

I am standing

where I have always stood.

(…silence)

SCENE IV — POLICY: THE LANGUAGE OF ORDER

Public speech enters. Words become tools. Fear is refined into policy. No one shouts. This is calm authority. The tension lies in how reasonable the division sounds. The moral temperature cools even as stakes rise.

INVOCATION

Flags.

Microphones.

Words arranged carefully.

Fear polished into policy.

REPORTER

Today the state announced expanded cooperation.

STATE OFFICIAL

Law without enforcement is suggestion.

Suggestion is weakness.

Weakness invites disorder.

We must draw a line.

MAYOR

And what does the line divide?

STATE OFFICIAL

Those who belong

and those who do not.

THE VOICE

You speak of belonging

as if it were a permit

instead of a human hunger.

MAYOR

You cannot govern a city

by teaching it to flinch.

STATE OFFICIAL

The public is afraid.

THE VOICE

You are treating fear

as if it were useful.

STATE OFFICIAL

Public safety is non-negotiable.

THE VOICE

Public dignity is not optional.

SCENE V — CAPTAIN MORROW: RITUAL BEFORE DUTY

Private preparation. The uniform is both armor and inheritance. The captain is not a villain; he is disciplined, methodical, tired. Fear has become procedural. Tone: steady, controlled, almost pastoral — but edged with fatigue.

INVOCATION

A kitchen table.

A uniform on a chair.

A child's drawing on the refrigerator.

Ritual before duty.

CAPTAIN MORROW

Shoes.

Belt.

Radio.

Keys.

The ritual is the prayer.

I have served this city

long enough to know

that fear has seasons.

It rises and falls

like weather.

But lately

fear has become the forecast.

They call it vigilance.

They call it preparedness.

They call it necessary.

(breath–pause)

Hold steady, I tell my hands.

Hold steady, I tell my men.

Hold the line.

Because if the line breaks,

the city thinks it dies.

And if the city thinks it dies,

it asks for harder answers.

(breath–pause)

I do not want to be the story.

But I have learned:

if you wear a uniform long enough

the uniform begins to wear you.

SCENE VI — OFFICER REYES: INHERITANCE

Conflict is internal before it is public. Reyes carries two loyalties that do not cancel each other. His struggle is quiet, not theatrical. The scene asks: What happens when obedience fractures identity?

INVOCATION

A bench under a streetlight.

A phone buzzing.

A mother's name in the caller ID.

A badge heavy on the chest.

OFFICER REYES

My father crossed a river

with one pair of shoes

and no English for mercy.

My mother cleans rooms

in a building

I am told to protect.

She empties trash

from offices

where people write words like "invasion."

She says,

"Be careful."

Not because I am a police officer—

because I am her son

and sons can be taken

by uniforms too.

(breath–pause)

Captain says: Hold.

The state says: Line.

The public says: Necessary.

And I stand here

between my mother's hands

and my own.

THE VOICE

Which hand will you obey

when both are trembling?

ACT II — THE LINE

SCENE VII — THE GATHERING

Energy rises. The city becomes audible. This is not chaos — it is compression. Hope and anger stand shoulder to shoulder. The line has not yet hardened. The actors must feel the fragile space before it becomes irreversible.

INVOCATION

Evening descends.

Courthouse steps fill.

Languages overlap.

A city listening to itself.

Breath tightening.

ELIJAH

Look up.

Look at what the city built.

Glass catching sun

and sending it back as glare.

Now look down—

at the hands that poured the concrete,

at the hands that wash the dishes,

at the hands that lift your elders

out of bed gently

and then go home

to be called unlawful.

This city runs on those hands.

ENSEMBLE (PROTESTORS, soft at first,

building)

No more raids.

No more cages.

No more disappearing.

DANIEL

(to someone beside him, quiet)

I just want to hear what they say.

(He edges slightly forward — not pushing, just trying to see.)

CAPTAIN MORROW

You have a permit until nine.

ELIJAH

Justice does not check the clock.

CAPTAIN MORROW

Justice does not throw bottles.

ELIJAH

Justice does not hide behind shields.

THE VOICE

The light of the body is the eye.

Take heed—

that your certainty

is not darkness

wearing a uniform.

SCENE VIII — THE LINE (Expanded)

Geometry becomes moral reality. Shields create shape; shape creates meaning. No one believes they are crossing a point of no return — yet they are. Tone: tightening. Breath shortens. The audience should feel proximity.

INVOCATION

Shields rise.

A line becomes a wall.

A wall becomes a lesson.

Noise tightening.

Hands in the air.

Hands misunderstood.

(The shields press. The crowd sways but does not break.)

CAPTAIN MORROW

Hold.

OFFICER REYES

Captain—

my mother is in this crowd

in every woman's face.

CAPTAIN MORROW

Keep your eyes forward.

OFFICER REYES

They are forward.

That's the problem.

(Breath—Pause. The crowd compresses.)

CAPTAIN MORROW

Forward.

(Reyes steps with the line. Focused. Controlled.)

OFFICER REYES

(quietly, to himself)

Watch the hands.

(He repeats it as doctrine.)

Watch the hands.

(A bottle shatters somewhere deep in the crowd — distant.

Sound only.)

OFFICER REYES

Movement — right side—

(He sees Daniel.)

DANIEL

(to someone beside him)

I'm not pushing —

I just can't see—

(He lifts his phone above shoulder height to record. One hand open.)

OFFICER REYES

(automatic cadence)

Unknown object.

(The crowd shifts. Daniel steadies himself, raising the phone higher.)

DANIEL

Mom —

I'm right here—

(Reyes' Breath tightens — not panic, compression.)

MEMORY — TRAINING LANGUAGE

(Ensemble, low, neutral, overlapping — procedural.)

Split second.

Perceived threat.

Close distance.

Necessary force.

(The light catches the phone's surface. A brief flash. Reyes does

not register it as a phone.)

OFFICER REYES

(whisper)

He's reaching—

DANIEL

I'm just trying to see—

(breath–pause.)

(Reyes fires. The shot is heard. Daniel falls.)

The line holds.

The body does not.

SCENE IX — THE SOUND

The moment collapses into a single irreversible act. No melodrama. No music. Only shock. The silence after the shot is the loudest presence in the room. Actors must trust stillness.

INVOCATION

A sound.

Then stillness.

(Daniel falls.)

No music.

No explanation.

Only Breath.

ELIJAH

Do not run.

Do not throw.

Do not give them the story

they are already writing.

CAPTAIN MORROW

Hold.

(voices overlap—*fear and chant*)

OFFICER (ENSEMBLE)

They're pushing—

CAPTAIN MORROW

Hold.

MIRIAM

He was looking.

(…long silence)

SCENE X — AFTER: THE HOPE THAT DOES NOT ERASE

Accountability begins, but clarity does not. Grief and justification occupy the same air. Hope is spoken carefully — not as consolation, but as condition. The scene breathes in fragments.

INVOCATION

Police lights paint the buildings.

Sirens approach like a tide.

A mother kneels.

A city holds its breath.

CAPTAIN MORROW

Who fired?

OFFICER REYES

I did.

(breath–pause)

CAPTAIN MORROW

Why?

OFFICER REYES

He moved—

I thought he was reaching—

I thought—

ELIJAH

For what do you fear

a boy's hand?

THE VOICE

Who taught you

to fear reaching?

(*...silence*)

THE VOICE

Looking is not the crime.

Looking is the beginning.

If you will not turn away.

Light remains

where it is welcomed.

(*...silence, then the world resumes*)

ACT III — NORMALIZATION

SCENE XI — THE STORY BECOMES A STORY

The event leaves the body and enters language. Distance grows. Certainty multiplies. The chorus becomes colder. Tone: clinical, procedural, media-smooth. The danger here is normalization.

INVOCATION

The story leaves the street.

It enters the air.

It multiplies.

It returns in fragments.

REPORTER

A teenager was shot tonight

during a protest downtown.

Authorities describe the scene as volatile.

STATE OFFICIAL

Our officers acted

to preserve order.

MAYOR

A life has been lost.

STATE OFFICIAL

There are consequences

for disorder.

THE VOICE

Consequences—

as if death were a fee

you pay to keep your fear.

ENSEMBLE *(as projected comments, spoken like a cold*

chorus)

Tragic but necessary.

He should have complied.

Both sides.

He had it coming.

Pray for the officers.

Pray for the family.

It's complicated.

THE VOICE

Complicated—

a word that means:

I will not look long enough

to change.

SCENE XII — CAPTAIN MORROW: REPORT LANGUAGE

Official memory is constructed. Words are selected to stabilize order. "Necessary" becomes a shield. The captain is aware of what language can do — and what it can conceal. This is confession without collapse.

INVOCATION

A desk lamp.

A blank form.

A pen that writes what the city will believe.

CAPTAIN MORROW

I can write the report.

I can say volatile.

I can say split-second.

I can say perceived threat.

And the words will work.

Words always work

if the audience is hungry for them.

(he looks outward)

Are you hungry?

(breath—pause)

They will ask me:

Was it necessary?

Necessary is a word

that makes blood ordinary.

Necessary is a word

spoken without tremor.

I said hold.

Not fire.

But I trained them

to hear movement as threat.

I fed them fear in small spoons

until fear became reflex

and reflex became doctrine.

We call it preparedness.

We call it safety.

We call it order.

THE VOICE

Order without mercy

is a clean room

with a locked door.

SCENE XIII — MIRIAM: THE PRIVATE ROOM

Public noise has faded. Grief is intimate now. The tone is raw but not hysterical. This is not spectacle; it is ache. The question shifts: What is a promise worth when it fails?

INVOCATION

A small apartment.

A school photo on the wall.

A hoodie on a chair.

A mother sitting because standing hurts.

MIRIAM

When he was little

he asked why the flag

was on the wall at school.

I told him

it was a promise.

A promise is a thing you hang up

so you can forget it

until you need it.

He believed it.

He believed this city was bright.

He believed it.

(breath–pause)

Now tell me:

What does citizen mean

when the street becomes courtroom

and the gun becomes gavel?

THE VOICE

Blessed are the ones

who still dare to look—

for they will grieve.

And grief is a form of love

that refuses denial.

SCENE XIV — THE MAYOR: THE WINDOW

Leadership stands at elevation. The skyline glows while consequence lingers below. The mayor balances survival and conscience. Tone: restrained, calculating, uneasy. The fear here is political — and moral.

INVOCATION

A window above the skyline.

The city shining like success.

Below: sirens and silence.

MAYOR

They want a statement.

They want balance.

They want me to say

I support the officers

and I mourn the boy—

as if language were a bridge

that can carry both

without cracking.

My staff says:

Do not inflame.

Do not provoke.

Do not lose donors.

Do not lose the next election.

Do not—

see too clearly.

(breath–pause)

A city does not die

when it is divided.

It dies

when it becomes accustomed

to division.

SCENE XV — THE HEARING THAT IS NOT A HEARING

Public testimony is permitted but contained. Time limits replace transformation. Truth surfaces accidentally. Tone: procedural civility masking deep fracture.

INVOCATION

Folding chairs.

Two-minute time limits.

A microphone that edits grief.

CLERGY (ENSEMBLE)

I have buried a child once.

I do not wish

to bury another

because someone called him

a threat.

CITIZEN 1 (ENSEMBLE)

I'm tired of fear.

CITIZEN 2 (ENSEMBLE)

I'm tired of crime.

CITIZEN 3 (ENSEMBLE)

My hotel would close in a week

without them.

(beat—truth slips out too casually)

THE VOICE

Listen:

dependence confessed

and still no welcome.

STATE OFFICIAL

We will not be lectured

by chaos.

ELIJAH

Chaos is not the crowd.

Chaos is a conscience

trained not to see.

SCENE XVI — THE SECOND NIGHT

Repetition. Rehearsal. The city prepares to reenact itself. Reyes is no longer steady. Morrow is more rigid. The line has become ritual. Tone: weary inevitability.

INVOCATION

More police.

More cameras.

More hunger for footage.

A city rehearsing itself.

CAPTAIN MORROW

No live rounds.

OFFICER (ENSEMBLE)

Yes, sir.

CAPTAIN MORROW

No heroics.

OFFICER (ENSEMBLE)

Yes, sir.

OFFICER REYES

Captain—

I can't—

CAPTAIN MORROW

You can.

You will.

You will stand.

That is what we do.

OFFICER REYES

That is what we do

until we cannot live with it.

(…silence)

THE VOICE

This is how the line becomes altar:

someone must fall

so the city can feel safe.

SCENE XVII — THE CROWD BECOMES THE STAGE

The audience is implicated. Watching is no longer passive. This scene feels uncomfortably direct. The actors are not accusing — they are exposing participation.

INVOCATION

House lights rise.

Faces visible.

No one hiding.

The city looking at itself.

REPORTER

You saw the clip.

You slowed it.

You zoomed.

You decided.

Eight seconds.

Three angles.

You said:

He moved too fast.

You said:

The officer feared for his life.

You said:

Both sides.

(breath–pause)

And then you ate dinner.

THE VOICE

You think you are watching.

You are practicing.

SCENE XVIII — CAPTAIN MORROW TO THE AUDIENCE

The captain speaks to the room without anger, returning the language of safety to those who asked for it. The line is no longer theory. It has weight. Policy has consequences.

INVOCATION

No front.

No backstage.

A circle of witnesses.

CAPTAIN MORROW

You told us the streets felt unsafe.

You told us the city was changing.

You told us: Draw the line.

We drew it.

He crossed it.

What did you expect?

(hold the silence)

Did you expect

a gentle hand on his shoulder?

Did you expect

a conversation?

Did you expect

your fear would remain metaphor

and not become metal?

I have watched this city

hire the invisible

and curse the invisible

and then ask them

to be grateful.

If you want a line—

understand what lines cost.

Lines cost bodies.

SCENE XIX — MIRIAM TO THE AUDIENCE

Presence without defense. A mother stands and refuses reduction. The room cannot retreat. Tone: quiet authority. Light becomes choice.

INVOCATION

A mother stands.

The room remains lit.

The city cannot pretend it is not present.

MIRIAM

He washed your dishes.

He stocked your shelves.

He studied for exams

in a break room.

He said, "yes ma'am."

to people who called him "boy."

He wanted to build bridges.

You did not see him

until you saw him fall.

(breath–pause)

Now you see me.

And you are deciding

what I am.

A mother?

A trespasser?

A worker?

A problem?

Say it.

Out loud.

(...silence)

(Then — she rises fully and moves — quietly

— into the stained-glass light.)

He believed this city was bright.

He believed it.

56

(breath–paus —quiet resolve)

Light remains

where it is welcomed.

(…silence)

SCENE XX — TAKE HEED

The word "Necessary" is held up and examined. Inflection becomes judgment. The final admonition is not shouted; it is offered. Silence is the last actor. No release. Only attention.

INVOCATION

The stained glass does not dim.

It does not look away.

It holds its light.

THE VOICE

Look at what we have seen.

Is it the word "**Necessary**"—

(breath–pause)

Spoken without memory —

without tremor.

(…silence)

THE VOICE

Take heed…

therefore

that the light which is in thee

be not darkness.

(…long silence—no movement)

No bow.

No curtain call.

The play ends in silence.

DIRECTOR'S STATEMENT

for the printed program

The Lamp is neither a protest play nor a sermon. It is a lament. It asks how a city sees—and what happens when fear begins to shape perception. The structure echoes scripture because conscience has always spoken in that register. The play unfolds in scenes because moral questions resist casual speech.

Performed in the round, the audience becomes part of the civic circle. There is no front. There is no safe distance. We see one another seeing.

The repeated line **"Light remains where it is welcomed"** is not reassuring. It is a condition. The final silence is intentional. Remain in it.

PLAYWRIGHT'S NOTE

This play stands in conversation with Archibald MacLeish's *J.B.* (1958), which reimagined the *Book of Job* for the twentieth century. If *J.B.* asked how faith survives catastrophe, *The Lamp* asks how conscience survives normalization.

AUDIENCE INVITATION

This work concludes without a cue for applause or musical release. You are invited to remain seated for a brief silence after the final words. Let the room remain visible. Let the light remain.

The play does not end in resolution. It ends in attention. Stay with what has been seen. If applause comes, let it arise naturally — not as dismissal of discomfort, but as acknowledgment of shared presence.

Stay with what has been seen.

APPENDIX

OPTION B Presentation
Scene XX – Civic Space Version

Remove stained glass reference entirely — make the theater
& stage the chapel. This version strips the ecclesial image and
makes illumination itself the theology.

SCENE XX — TAKE HEED

INVOCATION

The lights rise — not brighter, but clearer.
Faces visible.
No one hidden.
The room itself holds the light.

(…silence)

THE VOICE

Look at what we have seen.
It is the word "**Necessary**"—

(breath–pause)

Spoken without memory —
without tremor.

(…silence)

THE VOICE
Take heed…

therefore

that the light which is in thee

be not darkness.

(…long silence—no movement)

No bow.

No curtain call.

ABOUT THE AUTHOR

RON STARBUCK is the Publisher, CEO, and Executive Editor of Saint Julian Press. A poet and playwright, he is the author of six collections of poetry — *There Is Something About Being an Episcopalian, When Angels Are Born, Wheels Turning Inward, A Pilgrimage of Churches, At the Still Point: In Conversation with Saint Julian,* and *You Are Accepted: In Conversation with Paul Tillich.* He is also the author of *A White Colt's Tale,* a children's Christmas story, and the editor of *In My Father's House Are Many Mansions,* a collection of sermons by his clergy father spanning fifty years of ministry.

His work explores moral imagination, civic responsibility, and the contemplative tradition. *The Lamp* marks his first full-length play in verse, extending his poetic voice into the realm of civic drama.